REFERENCE NOR

RETURN TO DOWNTOWN

NO LONGER PROPERTY OF SPOKANE PUBLIC LIBRARY

VOICES OF
SEATTLE

Other books in this series

Voices of San Francisco

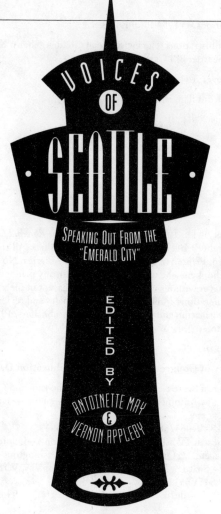

VOICES OF SEATTLE

SPEAKING OUT FROM THE "EMERALD CITY"

EDITED BY

ANTOINETTE MAY & VERNON APPLEBY

HarperCollins*West*

A Division of HarperCollins*Publishers*

Illustrations: © 1994 Philip Burke

Cover illustrations (clockwise): Jean Godden, Shawn Kemp, Chief Seattle, Bill Gates

Back cover: Ken Griffey, Jr.

Inside front flap: Richard Karn

Inside back flap: Jimi Hendrix

VOICES OF SEATTLE: *Speaking Out from the Emerald City*. Copyright © 1995 by HarperCollins Publishers. All rights reserved. Printed in the United States of America. No part of this book may be used or reproduced in any manner whatsoever without written permission except in the case of brief quotations embodied in critical articles and reviews. For information address HarperCollins Publishers, 10 East 53rd Street, New York, NY 10022.

FIRST EDITION

Library of Congress Cataloging-in-Publication Data:

Voices of Seattle : speaking out from the Emerald City / edited by Antoinette May and Vernon Appleby — 1st ed.
   p.   cm.
  ISBN 0–06–258584–3 (cloth: alk. paper)
   1. Seattle (Wash.)—Social life and customs—Quotations, maxims, etc. 2. Quotations, American—Washington (State)—Seattle. I. May, Antoinette. II. Appleby, Vernon.
 F899.S45V65 1995
 979.7'772—dc20   94–34980
                                          CIP

95 96 97 98 99 HAD 10 9 8 7 6 5 4 3 2 1

This edition is printed on acid-free paper that meets the American National Standards Institute Z39.48 Standard.

Contents

1   Ah! Wilderness   *1*

2   Seattleite Musings   *8*

3   Seattle Style   *14*

4   Business . . . as Usual?   *23*

5   Media Mix   *31*

6   Politics as Usual   *35*

7   Salmon Anxiety   *38*

8   Bon Appétit   *42*

9   Coffee Matters!   *45*

10   The First 150 Years   *52*

11   Will It Play in Seattle?   *60*

12   Grunge and Glory   *73*

13   Culture Still Survives   *81*

14   The Sporting Life   *83*

15   Rain . . . Who Needs an Umbrella?   *94*

16   Murder—They Wrote   *97*

17   In the Pits over Architecture   *102*

Chief Seattle had Thunderbird power.
It was made like a duck. That is how it would be
   shaken.
It would be shaken and the power of Seattle would be
   sung.
   Thunderbird was the power of Seattle.
   Thunderbird was the greatest power.
When Seattle would be angry at someone, he would
   shout angrily at him. The one he was angry at
   would shake.
   It was a big power, that power of Seattle.

Amelia Sneatlum, Squamish Elder

CHAPTER 1

Ah! Wilderness

Jim Hollman
Seattle writer

Despite what the fish and game department
likes us to believe about fishing, gardening
is easily the number one avocation in the
Pacific Northwest. Anyone who digs in the
earth probably ends up relating to slugs more
often than to any other wild animal in their lives.
We may treat the local Orca pods as wildlife
celebrities, we may reinvent the spotted owl as
our symbol of wildness, we may expend vast
amounts of money, time, and self-respect trying
to get close enough to grab a salmon under
the gills, but it is the slugs we know best.
And most often.

Slugs: our primary window into the
heart of the wilderness.

Chief Seattle
*On the occasion of an
early treaty
proposal*

It matters
little where
we pass the
remnant of
our days.
They will
not be many.
A few more moons,
a few more winters—
and not one of the
descendants
of the
mighty
hosts that
once moved
over this broad
land or lived in happy homes, protected by the Great
Spirit, will remain to mourn over the graves of a people
once more powerful and hopeful than yours. But why
should I mourn over the untimely fate of my people?
Tribe follows tribe, and nation follows nation, like the
waves of the sea. It is the order of nature, and regret is
useless. Your time of decay will be distant, but it will
surely come, for even the white man, whose God
walked and talked with him as friend with friend,
cannot be exempt from the common destiny.
We may be brothers, after all. We will see.

Betty MacDonald
*Referring to the Olympic Peninsula,
which would inspire her comic classic
The Egg and I*

. . . the most rugged, most westerly, deepest, largest,
wildest, gamiest, richest, most fertile, loneliest, and
most desolate country in the world.

~~~~~~~~~~

Andy Stahl
Environmental forester

Now, my dentist
is not an environmentalist,
but when I heard her say
her heart ached when she
watched big trucks rumble
down the road filled
with giant trees, it was
enough for me to determine
we had public support.
People like big trees and
they don't realize that until
they see them being threatened . . .
One thing I do regret is that the
environmental organizations
have been no more
forward-looking and helpful
in finding economic
solutions than anyone else.

Jean Godden
Seattle Times
columnist

Real Puget Sounders
call Mount Rainier
"The Mountain."
On a clear day
they say,
"The Mountain is out."

~~~~~~~

Darlene Madenwald
Washington
Environmental Council
President

I can see how
other people can be
driven to lie down
on train tracks to stop
nuclear shipments . . .
It's just a matter
of being human—
one aspect of our work
that we all too often forget.
By being too rigid,
it's easy to get
stunned by the
"jobs versus trees"
complaint.

Harriet Bullitt
Former owner and partner,
with her sister,
of King Broadcasting

Our grandfather started a sawmill
and helped to clear-cut Ballard.
And he gained wealth here.
He was a very aggressive,
hard-nosed businessman. . . .
Now our generation is very
much into nonprofit and
here we are operating a
foundation giving away
as much money as we can to
save the forests that my
grandfather did not cut.

~~~~~~~

Dr. Tag Gornall
Of the Marine Animal
Resource Center

Eating the sea bottom, which is rich
in nutrients from matter that dies at the top
and sinks, can be like licking the cake bowl.
But if ships hauling aluminum illegally
wash out their holds or the whale stops
to eat outside the dumping grounds
of former factories, it's like licking
the bottom of the toilet bowl.

Casey Sander
Costar of ABC's
"Grace Under Fire"
and a Seattleite

The Northwest is
the most beautiful
place in the world
and please don't hate
Californians for
coming up here.
Everyone comes to
their senses sometime.

~~~~~

Steve Johnston
Seattle Times reporter

Anyone who has
lived in the Northwest
for more than a year
knows what happens
when it rains and
then the sun comes out
and then it rains
and so on.
Morning glories
(better known by
their Latin name:
Plantus From Hell)
spring up.

John Doerper
Seattle writer

Anglers are romantics.
 Otherwise they wouldn't be here, braving
   the morning chill as they hold mugs of
    hot coffee in cupped hands, standing around
   waiting to load their gear, talking.
Wherever you join a group of fishermen,
  whether on river, lake, or coast,
    you'll note a singular camaraderie,
      fostered by the single-mindedness
       of the pursuit, enhanced by the
         knowledge that you might need to
          ask for help from or render aid to the
        man or woman standing next to you.
   He or she might be a stranger in real life,
  perhaps an accountant or a computer
 programmer, but here, in the dreamlike world
of the fishing grounds, he or she might be a
comrade. Perhaps this is the real reason
 charter fishing is such a popular sport.
   It's not the fish that matter—
     you can buy them cheaper from the
      ritziest fishmonger in town.

CHAPTER 2
Seattleite Musings

Ann L. McClure
Seattle office worker

I sympathize with the gardeners here in the
Pacific Northwest (since I love my pansies), but
reading stories of how slugs are losing their insides
on various concoctions we dream up for them doesn't
do much for teaching our children to love the
environment and all its critters. But seeing a child's
(or adults's) face after they have been "kissed" by a
slug—that's something. It isn't exactly "kissing."
What you do is find a slug happily going along your
sidewalk, get down to "slug level," and put your finger
down in front of him. He stops in his tracks, sniffs
your finger, wiggles his nose, and, if you're lucky,
he puts out his tongue to your finger and "kisses" it.
So when you get frustrated with those little critters,
relax and realize we have to share the environment.
Get down to "Slugville" and maybe you'll get a kiss.

Charles Johnson
*Seattle writer and recipient of
the 1990 National Book Award for
his novel Middle Passage*

I think there's such a thing
as spirit of place. Some people think
because of the rain that Seattle is moody.
But I think I'm moody,
so it fits me perfectly.

～～～～～

Donny Marrow
Producer of Seattle's Muzak recordings

It's not so much that principles change . . .
I'm just happy and grateful to be doing
the things I said I would *never* do.

～～～～～

Jimi Hendrix
*World-renowned guitarist and
Seattle native, in 1970*

A couple of years ago,
all I wanted was to be heard.
"Let me in!" was the thing.
Now, I'm trying to figure out
the *wisest* way to be heard.

Peg Phillips
Seattle resident and storekeeper Ruth-Anne
on the CBS television series "Northern Exposure"

I get fan mail that's sometimes
embarrassing because they say,
"Ruth-Anne, you're an inspiration to me."
I don't know how in the hell
I'm an inspiration to anybody.
But it's usually after they read
that I went back to school at sixty-five,
which I don't consider
anything unusual at all.
It just took me fifty years
to realize my dream . . .

Angelo Pellegrini
Author and professor emeritus
at the University of Washington

I am not Dante, but when I courted my Beatrice,
I knew no less than he, that I was transfigured by
l'amor che move il sole e l'altre stelle. That was fifty-six
years ago. We are now old and gray and we sleep well.
Perhaps we are such stuff as dreams are made on;
but our little life is not rounded by a sleep.

Bill Gates
*Chief executive and cofounder
of Seattle's Microsoft, the largest
software company in the world*

I'm very well grounded because
of my parents and my job and
what I believe in. Some
people ask me why I don't
own a plane, for instance.
Why? Because you can get
used to that kind of stuff,
and I think that's bad.
It takes you away from
normal experiences in
a way that is
probably
debilitating.
So I control
that kind of
thing
intentionally.
If my
discipline
ever broke
down, it
would
confuse
me.

Wayne Johnson
Seattle men's activist and therapist

Men are getting tired of being nice guys.
Many men have reached the point where
they feel they've been too nice, accepted
too much, been overwhelmed by a barrage of
talk shows and media outlets that depict men
as the enemy. . . . Men as stupid, insensitive
male chauvinist pigs. We men who are getting
active are saying, "We've had enough."

~~~~~~~

Anonymous
Seattle resident

What's this deal with the Pacific Northwest?
Is there an Atlantic Northwest?
People in the Northeast don't say they live
in the Atlantic Northeast.
Why can't we just drop the Pacific?
It's redundant!

~~~~~~~

Catherine Skinner
Artist and civic volunteer

In terms of race relations,
Seattle is one of the most exciting
places to be right now.
It's not like L.A. The hate isn't here.

Dr. Michael Copass
*Director of emergency services
at Harborview Medical Center,
a training facility for the
University of Washington
School of Medicine*

It's a fragile business,
teaching people how to
take care of other people.
It's not something that is
done in a book.
We do it in the most
dramatic setting of all . . .

~~~~~~~~~

Anonymous
Seattle native

Most of my friends in Seattle,
if given the choice
between meeting and
shaking hands with the
Pope or Bill Clinton,
would choose the Dalai Lama.

CHAPTER 3
Seattle Style

New Yorker magazine
In a cartoon about Seattle

They're backpacky,
but nice.

Archie Binns
Author and historian

Seattle started in isolation as
complete as that of Plymouth, Massachusetts;
and in the process of surviving and growing,
its citizens developed hardihood and enterprise,
a remarkable capacity for community action,
and a spirit of undefeated youth.

Michele Matassa Flores
Writer and Seattle native

People today pay hundreds of thousands of dollars
   for views like the one that disappeared from
      Denny Hill. They add entire wings onto
         their houses to capture one more mountain,
            lake, or skyscraper.
And they fight—oh, do they fight—
   when new waves of view-lovers move
      into their line of sight.
            Or should that be sights?
What would Denny
   [Seattle founder Arthur Denny]
      think if he could rise today to witness:
         One man who worked after dark to enlarge
            his house for a view of the mountains.
               He couldn't get a building permit,
                  so he moved walls a foot at a time
                  night after night
                     hoping neighbors
                        wouldn't notice the change.
A couple who planted fir trees to block their
   neighbors' view. They had been told they
      couldn't add on to their house because
         neighborhood rules protected views.
            But rules regarding landscaping are
               vague, so the couple planted fir trees
                  that blocked the view,
                     then claimed the neighbors had
                        no view to protect.

Linda Evans
Actress and former
Seattle resident

As for dressing up,
when I recently had
to wear a proper
dress and high heels,
I had them sent up
from Beverly Hills.
I came up here
to get away from
the Hollywood
scene. This
place makes
my heart sing.

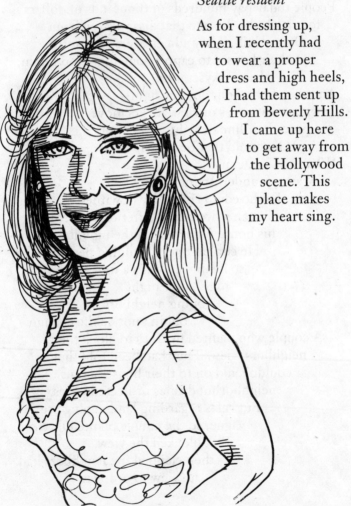

Jim Hollman
Writer and Seattle resident

Many a morning in June I've come upon slugs
three feet up on my asparagus plants, rocking
back and forth in the feathery foliage
like a sailor relaxing on a hammock.

Paula Head
Concierge at Seattle's Westin Hotel

There's something about the Northwest geography
that overwhelms people, confuses them.
"What pier do I go to to take the ferry to Alaska?"
they'll ask, or "Where do I get the monorail to
Bellevue?" How many times have I explained that
there is no bridge to Victoria?

Maureen Neal
Sales manager at Seattle's Vintage Park Hotel

I think the Seattle ambience relaxes people—
like the man who felt so comfortable that he
wandered down to the lobby every morning of
his stay wearing a bathrobe and slippers, chatting
cheerily with the other guests over his morning coffee.
Another guest who climbed out on the fire escape in
his boxers to enjoy a morning cigarette, only to have
the door lock behind him, wasn't quite so perky.

Kate Bornstein (formerly Al)
Author of Gender Outlaw,
describing life after
her girlfriend Catherine
became her boyfriend David

I've always been attracted to women,
but being one was not all that I
bargained on. I'd get to the store with
David, and they'd always talk to him.
They ignored me.
If we went to the restaurant together,
they talked to him, not me.
I came from a position of power,
being a white boy.
The reality of the change was stunning—
the reality of becoming
a second-class citizen,
of being objectified by men.

~~~~~~~~

Bruce Pavitt
Cofounder and partner
in Seattle's Sub Pop Records

When somebody associates
someone with being a resident
of the Pacific Northwest,
there's a lot of Paul Bunyan
notions of people
raising Cain out in the hills.

Jean Godden
Seattle Times columnist

Seattleites are apt to cultivate beards,
wear hiking boots or running shoes with their
business suits, and get a speeding ticket in the
Arboretum. They seldom visit the Space Needle,
seldom exhibit décolletage or expanses of skin,
seldom smile spontaneously while walking
(basically they're shy), seldom ride the Monorail,
and seldom wear husband-wife look-alike outfits.

~~~~~~

Tom Kelly
Real estate consultant

Feng-shui men and women,
sometimes known as geomancers,
advise that sofas, chairs, and desks
face the doorway, even if you have to
give up a dynamite view of Puget Sound.
The key is to design the home so that
the doorway and any possible view
co-mingle.

~~~~~~

Eric Lenard
*Hunt Club chef and San Francisco transplant,
discussing what surprised him most about Seattle*

Your drivers all seem to be on tranquilizers.

Connie Mackenzie
*Who gave up a 3,000-square-foot Dutch Colonial
to live on a 400-square-foot house barge
on Lake Union*

This is the most fun place to live . . .
to think that in 400 feet we have a shower,
a vanity sink, a fireplace, and a sliding patio door—
all the things that houses have.

~~~~~~~~

Cal Anderson
*Washington State Representative,
while posing for a campaign photo before
the "Waiting for the Interurban" statue*

It was a mob scene.
Not only opening day of yachting season,
but just before the Sonics' game.
We had to stop traffic to take the pictures.
But even though it was one of
the busiest days of the year,
no one honked.

~~~~~~~~

Mae West
"First Lady" of Seattle's famous Market

I only like two kinds of men—
foreign and domestic.

Anonymous
Seattle resident

Traffic snarls? Mellowness?
   Part of the problem is
      the passiveness of the drivers.
         How about when there are
            fifteen cars in line at the stoplight,
         it turns green, the lead car crawls out,
      and only five cars make it across before
   the light turns red again? . . .
How about those mellow drivers
   cruising at fifty miles per hour
      in the fast lane?
         It's as if all the drivers in Seattle
            are on Valium.

~~~~~~~

Mindy Cameron
Seattle writer

It's summer, it's hot,
   you work in the city
and you want to have a little fun
   over your lunch break.
      You take a walk, buy
         an iced latte, go shopping,
      maybe catch an outdoor concert
   or find a quiet spot to sit and read.
That's all very nice, but is it really *fun*?
Or is it just being sedate in Seattle?

Smart Money magazine

People go out of their way to be polite in Seattle.
Ask directions and likely as not a perfect stranger
will offer to walk you to your destination.

~~~~~

Norm Langill
Founder of One Reel Festivals

Seattle's a wonderful town because
it's on the frontier between Asia and Europe.
Here, nobody has clear turf control over the city.
We could be Tokyo East or Paris West—
we are an intersection of those two cultures.

~~~~~

Jean Godden
Seattle Times columnist

A Seattle native is a Californian,
Minnesotan, or Iowan who has lived
in Seattle more than six months and knows
how to pronounce Sequim (or Puyallup).

~~~~~

San Francisco Examiner

Seattle is an old gold-mining stopover peopled by
too many boring Canadians to have any real style.

CHAPTER 4

Business ... as Usual?

~~~~~~~~

Lloyd Nelson
*Entrepreneur, recalling the 1920 birth in Seattle of
his first mass-produced backpack—the Trapper Nelson*

I joined the throngs of miners, fishermen,
and other footloose Alaskans who were staking
claims on newly opened oil-reserve land.
While I was assembling an outfit to enable me
to cross a mountain range on foot, an Indian
agreed to lend me his crude packboard made of seal
skins stretched over willow sticks, a style used for
generations by his ancestors. I made the trip
and staked my claim but afterwards lay awake
nights recalling the backbreaking ordeal and
wondering if it would be possible to evolve
a really comfortable backpacking device.

Andrea Riniker
Sea-Tac Airport director

This expanding capacity is what fires me up.
The fun part in doing business in the public sector is
the responsibility to educate and persuade.

~~~~~~~~~

Paul Andrews
Seattle Times technology reporter

If a great idea needs a
great name to achieve
immortality, desktop
publishing proved to
be a term for the ages.
It was more poetic than
"word processing" or
"spreadsheet," less opaque
than "multimedia" and
"virtual reality." It became
to the personal computer
what the theory of relativity
is to physics and rock 'n' roll
is to adolescence—a term
expressing not just a
concept but a culture.

Craig McCaw
Founder and CEO
of McCaw Cellular
Communications
in the Seattle
area

Something
as catastrophic as
the original Ice Age
is coming to
telecommunications . . .
by ICE, I mean the
convergence of
Information, Computers,
and Entertainment.

Paul Brainerd
Seattle entrepreneur,
speaking to a group of venture capitalists

Why don't we call it desktop publishing?

Later explaining, as its inventor

It was the best thing I could think of.

To his mother, VerNetta Brainerd

I'll either be very rich by the time I'm forty,
or I'll be very poor.

Her reply

I'm very supportive of you,
but I hope you'll be very rich.

And today

We want him to enjoy his money.
We certainly have.

Bruce Nordstrom
*President of Seattle-based Nordstrom,
which would become the largest-volume
apparel store on the West Coast, in 1973*

It's really meaningful that someone
is spending a lot of time, money, and sweat
to do something for downtown.
We can build suburban stores forever
and they will be successful.
But this—by a mile—
is the biggest thing we ever did.

~~~~~~~~~

Greg Heberlein
Seattle Times columnist

Boeing truly is an enigma, an unsolved problem.
On the one hand, it is
the pillar of the community,
the provider through
its massive payroll of
more kids' bikes, family vacations, and
college educations than anyone
within 800 miles.
On the other, it is the 800-pound gorilla
that surreptitiously stalks
the befuddled little bureaucrat,
poised to pounce
should the government as much as
blink at the hue of the lavatory sign.

Bruce Poneman
*Cofounder and partner
of Seattle's Sub Pop Records*

If people enjoy coming to work,
then they don't ask for as much pay. The use of ironic
humor is the glue that bonds the company together,
because if you can't have a good laugh once in awhile,
you might as well be working at Boeing.

———~~~———

Lawrence Clarkson
Vice president of Seattle-based Boeing Company

We're working on systems to permit airplanes to land
no matter how bad the fog. With virtual reality and
some other things we're doing, I can see being able to
land with perfect safety in zero/zero conditions.

———~~~———

Bill Gates
*Cofounder of Seattle's Microsoft Company,
describing his boyhood*

People thought I was a goof-off, a class clown at
times. . . . Then I went to private school, and there was
no position called the clown. . . . In fact, I didn't have
clear positioning for a couple of years. I was trying
the no-effort-makes-a-cool-guy routine.
When I did start trying, people said,
"Whoa, we thought he was stupid! Better reassess."

Scott Oki
*University of Washington regent
and former Microsoft executive*

I call it learning on demand.
When we really have full interactivity
wherever you are, when you can be receiving and
sending signals and interacting at a very high
bandwidth—would one need classrooms?

New Yorker *magazine*

To many people, the rise of Bill Gates marks the
revenge of the nerd. Actually, Gates probably
represents the end of the word nerd as we know it.

Fortune *magazine*

CEO Bill Gates could buy out an entire year's
production of his ninety-nine nearest competitors,
burn it, and still be worth more than Rupert
Murdoch or Ted Turner. Microsoft's
$25 million market value tops that
of Ford, General Motors, 3M,
Boeing, RJR Nabisco,
General Mills,
Anheuser-Busch,
or
Eastman Kodak.

Norm Langill
Founder of One Reel Festivals

We're an international city
    whether we think so or not.
        Eventually, we had to ask how
            Bumbershoot could help Seattle,
    put it on the map.
Japan, for instance, has always
    used culture as a tool of trade.
        We're not merchants *of* culture,
        but we are certainly
merchants *with* culture.

Paul Brainerd
Seattle entrepreneur, discussing his business start as a
boy working in his father's camera shop

There was this whole idea of the direct link
between providing service to the customer,
    coming back, paying the grocery bill,
paying off the loan, being able to go on vacation.
    So you're part of this bigger system.
I'm really thankful for that, because I think
a lot of people in my generation were really
disconnected from understanding the basics of
business and the way the world worked.

CHAPTER 5
Media Mix

~~~~~~~

Charles Johnson
Seattle writer
and recipient of the 1990 National Book Award
for his novel Middle Passage

During each writing project I rethink every thought
I've ever had and reevaluate every feeling I've ever had.
I approach every novel or short story as if it might be
the very last thing I ever say to anybody.

~~~~~~~

Emmett Watson
Seattle Times columnist
(a.k.a. "Mr. Seattle")

I like Californians.
When I'm down there.

Jim French
Seattle talk-show host

When I got started in radio long ago,
I was taught that you are quite literally
a guest in people's homes or in their cars.
You do nothing to insult them or offend them.
I have gotten so used to doing that,
it would be unnatural for me to change.

~~~~~~~

Debbie Tomassi
Creator of the cartoon "Gladys"
and Seattle resident

I always thought, I can't write,
but they're sending me paychecks!
This is such a competitive field,
how could I be making it?
But I've just kept doing it until
somebody told me I can't and
nobody has told me I can't yet.

~~~~~~~

Gladys
Cartoon character

Inside this body
is a thin person just
screaming to get out . . .
I ate her.

Kelsey Grammer
As Seattle radio shrink,
Frasier,
in the CBS television
series "Frasier"

The mark of a man
is one who knows he can't
control his circumstances—
but he can control his
responses.

N. G. Assunta
*Editor and publisher
of Seattle's Northwest Asian Weekly*

To start the immigrant dream,
you begin from nothing and then
have some sort of empire.
I'm creating a little empire . . .
It's important that we have a
diversified perspective,
because many times
we see things from the
Asian perspective,
and don't see things from the
mainstream perspective.

~~~~~~~~~

San Francisco Examiner

Seattle dwellers always talk
about going back as if the burg
were some sort of Mecca.
The stay-put locals seem
content enough in their
pretty little environment.
There must be drugs
in the water.

CHAPTER 6
Politics as Usual

Peter von Reichbauer
Former Senator turned Metropolitan
King County Council Budget Chief

I don't want my epitaph to say,
"He served, but nobody knows what he did."
It should say, "He worked hard."

Joni Balter
Political columnist,
about von Reichbauer

It could say, "He worked hard
and drove everyone else nuts."

Rob Taylor
Post-Intelligencer reporter

Log-hungry timber companies
    and their allies are deploying a new weapon
        in Washington's timber wars:
            framing the conflict as owls versus schools.
The timber industry, having lost repeated battles
    for federal trees, has turned to demanding
        more timber sales from state "school trust"
          lands, which are managed to produce
            cash for school construction.
The industry's message: By shrinking timber sales
    to spare wildlife, the state is taking classrooms
        away from schoolchildren.

Charles Rice
Surgeon, discussing graphic photographs in his
Harborview Medical Center office that depict children
rushed to the hospital with gunshot wounds

Someday I'll put them together in a collage
and call them my NRA poster children . . .
In trauma, sooner or later, you butt up against
public-policy issues. People say guns don't kill
people, bullets do. That's true. If I were to attack
this as a public-policy issue, I'd put an enormous
tax on bullet manufacturers. Make guns cheap,
but bullets enormously expensive.

John Baden
Chairman of the Foundation for Research on
Economics and the Environment

In politics, duplicity accompanies opportunism
and honorable behavior is a severe liability.
Honorable politicians are like vegetarian coyotes
in that they face a great handicap when
competing with their red-meat opponents.

Booth Gardner
Governor of Washington
in his 1991 State of the State address,
describing environmentalist
Darlene Madenwald

Environmentalists may be hell to live with,
but they make great ancestors.

Darlene Madenwald
Washington Environmental Council President
(known as the "Velvet Steamroller")

If you think you're too small to be effective,
you've never been to bed with a mosquito.

CHAPTER 7

Salmon Anxiety

John Marshall
Post-Intelligencer reporter

Now the frightening headlines come day after day,
with words like "crisis" and "emergency" and
"endangered," all attached to salmon. And suddenly,
what had seemed a Northwest birthright—
salmon in our ocean waters, salmon in our rivers,
salmon on our plates—is called into serious question
for the first time. The result: A growing Salmon
Anxiety among eaters in this region.

Emmett Watson
Seattle Times columnist and curmudgeon laureate

I've lived here all my life and I never caught a salmon.
I do *not* commune with nature.

Tom Douglas
Chef of the Dahlia Lounge restaurant

I have seriously considered whether I should only buy
farmed salmon on philosophical grounds and not
participate at all in the wild salmon catch.

———

Susan Phinney
Food writer

Salmon.
It might as well be Seattle's middle name.

———

Jon Rowley
*Food consultant,
saluting residents for their
piscine sophistication*

People here are fish-smart and salmon-smart.

———

Wayne Ludvigsen
Food director for Ray's Boathouse

People do ask about salmon now
and that was never an issue
until a couple of years ago.
So we have become very specific these days
about where our salmon is coming from.

Sally McArthur
Executive chef for Anthony's Restaurant

All our waitpeople took classes which explained that wild fish are still plentiful in Alaska, Canada, and some rivers on the Pacific Coast. Anthony's is committed to preserving salmon and purchases fish only from healthy runs. We told our staff not to worry that they would ever have to serve the last salmon from some endangered run.

Kathy Fletcher
Executive director of People of Puget Sound

As Puget Sound goes, so go the salmon. From the time they hatch high up in the watershed where logging practices have destroyed and damaged much of the good spawning area, young salmon move down through farmland where animals and agricultural runoff degrade the streams, through increasingly large areas of suburbanization and urban area where land development paves over the landscape and alters streams and rivers forever.

Senator Patty Murray

We are at a crucial point. I vote for the salmon. We may not be able to recover salmon stocks regionwide, but I believe we have a cultural, moral, and legal obligation to try.

John Hinterberger
Seattle food writer

It looks like a fish market should look.
    It is situated where a fish market should be,
it even has a solid, fish market kind of name—
a name with, if you will, fish market ethics.
The Wild Salmon fish market holds forth at
Fishermen's Terminal on Salmon Bay,
    a few dozen feet from Seattle's
        home port fishing fleet.
            And, as a matter of principle,
                it sells what it says it sells—wild salmon.
            If it was raised on a fish farm,
        it is not sold there.
            If it grew up gulping pellets,
                it is not sold there.
The Wild Salmon sells nothing
    that has served time
        in involuntary confinement,
        in pond-reared servitude
            or two years in the pen.
            A statement to that effect
                is posted in the front window.
            In support of local and Alaskan fishermen,
                the sign says the Wild Salmon
                    sells only fish caught by
                American fishermen.
            In the wild:
    no drugs, no additives,
        no nonsense.

CHAPTER 8
Bon Appétit

Steve Pool
KOMO's television weather reporter
and host of Seattle's nationally syndicated
"Front Runners" program

I tend to lean toward restaurants that are somewhat
out of the mainstream—small, funky places that not
everyone knows about. I like developing a
relationship with the owner and being able to talk to
the chef who's preparing my meal, like I do at Seleh.
Another of my favorites is Ristorante Buongusto
on Queen Anne. I've known the owner for years and
I go there all the time. I like to sit at a little table
back by the bar, where I can relax and not be
asked what the weather's going to be like tomorrow.
Not that I mind that, usually—it's just kind of
hard to talk when you have minestrone dripping
down your chin.

Watts Wacker
Food futurist

Seattle, in my take, is an emerging city
that could end up being not only one
of the world-class cities in this country,
but *the* world-class city in this country.

~~~~~~~~~~~

Susan Phinney
Seattle food writer

Slug butter. It's not only a protein.
It's a fruit spread made with either
a pear or apple base, and priced from $5 to $7.
If anyone asks why it's called "slug butter," just say
the Pacific Northwest is so full of the slimy things
somebody had to do something with them.

~~~~~~~~~~~

Tom Douglas
Chef of the Dahlia Lounge restaurant

I have the coolest stove around.
It's a '52 Wedgewood with lots of chrome . . .
a six-burner gas range, a big one. I looked all over
the West Coast for one. Cost? It cost $700 to buy it,
another $200 to ship it up here, and another $200
to recondition it, and I did all the work myself.
I'm proud of that little puppy . . .
It's just like Mum's.

Jeff Smith
The PBS "Frugal Gourmet"

Pity the people
who hide their equipment.
If everything's all hidden
and your kitchen looks
like some kind of
veterinarian's surgery ward,
there's no inspiration.
I want a kitchen to say
"Please use me" when you walk in . . .
and don't ever cook
with electricity.
It's like trying to make
love to a Methodist.

~~~~~~~~

Joyce Taylor
KING-TV news anchor

I'm a little bit klutzy,
but when I'm cooking
it's really bad.
I move so fast that,
in a smaller kitchen,
I couldn't have anyone
around me.
They'd probably get hurt.

CHAPTER 9

Coffee Matters!

~~~~~~

Bart Becker
Contributing editor, Greater Seattle

Obviously, high-octane coffee
is more readily available in Seattle than
in just about any other city you can name.
Those of us who live here take it for granted
until we find ourselves in some distant burg,
staring gloomily into a cup of water-brown liquid.
You call this coffee? You call this a *city*?
But latte-mania has produced a mutant growth
pattern, and Seattle has become a self-parody
of caffeine consumption. It's the place you
can buy espresso everywhere—
from Eagle Hardware to
Archie McPhee's kitsch store . . .
and the place with a clinic called Espresso Dental.

Elayne Boosier
Comedienne
and frequent Seattle visitor

Seattle is
an old Native American term for *latte*.

~~~~~

Paula Bock
Pacific magazine staff writer

Being a barista, making decent coffee, takes skill.
    If you're good, you adjust your burr grinders
        with every cup through the morning sun
            and humidity rise.
Espresso is temperamental stuff.
    You've got to find the right rhythm to grind,
        flip, tamp, brush, shove, twist,
            jerk, jiggle, swipe, swirl, chat
                while you're really thinking
            about your sister's new used motorcycle
and hauling a secondhand
        refrigerator after work.

~~~~~

Laura Moix
Seattle's Starbucks coffee spokeswoman

We would be hard-pressed to name any country
    in the world that hasn't contacted us.
We had a call from Egypt the other day . . .

Mayor Norman B. Rice
*Declaring Seattle's
Special Coffee Week*

Whereas the people
of Seattle have
become inseparably
fond of high-quality
specialty coffee and
have crafted a vibrant
and growing industry
around it . . .

Dave Olsen
Chief coffee buyer at Starbucks

We didn't invent coffee.
We just started paying it some attention.

~~~~~~~~~~

Corby Kummer
Writer for New York magazine

Seattle *needed* coffee. It rains all the time
and people had to figure out some way to
stay awake during the long gray days. Also,
at least before the invasion of Californians
and Easterners, Seattle natives were strangely
easygoing and friendly. They could stand
a little caffeine, maybe even a lot.

~~~~~~~~~~

Dr. Ernesto Illy
Italian chemist and coffee roaster,
discussing the role of the baristas
in Seattle culture

Opening the small bars,
interacting with the consumer is
becoming a beautiful process in Seattle.
People are looking for *who*
is behind the machines . . .
He is not a movie star,
but he is a little star.

Jean Godden
_Seattle
Times
columnist_

Real Puget Sounders experience withdrawal if they haven't had a double-tall by midmorning. Their worst nightmare would be an espresso spill while traveling Interstate 5 to Tacoma.

Real visitors ask baristas for "a cup of coffee." They think Puget Sounders have gone a bit wacko over coffee. They complain that coffee here tastes "burned." They ask, "Don't you have any Maxwell House?"

Paula Bock
Pacific magazine staff writer

Of twentysomething baristas in Seattle, 96 percent wear black on *and* off the job; 99 percent hate fluorescent light and office cubicles. Your corner barista pulls 230 shots a day and earns $9,000 a year . . . This April, Paradiso taped a slip of paper to the cafe door—Experienced Barista Needed—and got 36 applications in three days.

~~~~~~

Judith Blak
Reporter, about the fancy-coffee capital of the world

A trip down a local supermarket's coffee aisle tells the tale. First, you're hit with the rich aroma of whole beans—Sumatra, Italian Roast, Dark Colombian, etc. Then you see that the whole-bean section has swelled—to twenty feet in some stores—while the canned section has shrunk.

~~~~~~

Anonymous

I think people in Seattle drink far too much coffee. It's affecting their attitudes and it's affecting other people's lives, everyone drives erratically.
You need to decaf yourselves, folks.

The Lingo of Latte Land

Latte: a shot of espresso
with steamed milk,
topped with
foamed milk.

Grande: a sixteen-ounce
latte.

Tall Skinny:
a tall latte
made with
nonfat milk.

No Fun: a latte
made with
decaffeinated
espresso.

Double No Fun:
a double latte
made with
decaf espresso.

Caffe Mocha:
chocolate syrup
or hot chocolate
with a shot of espresso
and steamed milk.

Thunder Thighs: a double tall
mocha made
with whole milk
and topped with
extra whipped cream.

CHAPTER 10

The First 150 Years

———————

"Grandma Fay"
Early pioneer,
tells of the landing of the Seattle pilgrims

I can't never forget the folks landed at Alki Point.
I remember it rained awful hard that last day—
    and the starch got took out of our bonnets
and the wind blew, and when the women
    got into the rowboat to go ashore
        they were crying every one of 'em,
            and their sunbonnets with the starch took
        out them went flip flap, flip flap,
            as they rowed off for shore,
and the last glimpse I had of them
    was the women standing under the trees
        with their wet bonnets all lopping down
over their faces and their aprons in their eyes.

Arthur Denny
Founder of Seattle, describing his arrival

I had gone a step too far . . .
it was not until I became aware that my wife and
helpless children were exposed to the murderous
attacks of hostile savages that it dawned upon me
that I had made a desperate venture. My motto in
life was never to go backward . . . I had brought my
family from a good home, surrounded by comforts
and luxuries, and landed them in a wilderness, and I
did not think it at all strange that a woman who had,
without complaint, endured all the dangers and
hardships of a trip across the great plains, should
be found shedding tears when contemplating the
hard prospects then so plainly in view.

Evelyn Hoffman
*Historian, recounting the life
of her great-grandmother in 1854*

During that first winter when they lived
in a log house open at one end, they would hang
heavy blankets over the opening at night, but the
unchinked logs still left room for plenty of breeze
where the wolves would press their noses, sniffing
the pungent aromas of the food in the cabin. On
hearing the wolves outside, the children would take
turns heating the poker in the wood coals and
thrusting it expertly on wolf noses. This action, of
course, caused the wolves to beat a hasty retreat.

Archie Binns
Author and historian

He [Dr. David S. Maynard] also had a name
for the city. He proposed that it be named after
his friend and fishing companion, Chief Seattle.
Thanks to the pioneering doctor, Seattle was
born with a fish-packing industry, a drugstore
and a general store, and a name that was not
imported from England or Spain or brought
around the Horn from the East.
It was a name as native as the fir tree.

~~~~~~~~~~

New York Times
On the Mercer Girls,
women recruited
from Massachussetts
by Seattle pioneer Asa Mercer
to settle in Seattle

But whoever they are,
and whensoever they come,
it is certain that those gentle
pioneers go out to the West
with a high sense of purpose
to which they are devoted, and
with hopes educated and purified
by the adversities attendant
upon the efforts of women
at self-help in the East.

Springfield Republican
About the Mercer Girls

. . . and it may well be doubted
whether any girl who goes
to seek a husband is worthy
to be a decent man's wife,
or is ever likely to be.

———〜〜〜———

Ida May Barlow Pinkham
A Mercer Girl

Each day of the trip passed uneventfully,
the only serious calamity happened
on the second day out when one of
the girls lost her false teeth overboard
in a moment of anguish rather common
to travelers on the ocean, and for
three months until we reached
San Francisco, she was called toothless.

———〜〜〜———

A Mercer Girl
*Describing the city's bachelors
who came to meet her,
in 1864*

Looking like grizzlies in store clothes
and their hair slicked down like otters.

Asa Mercer
Responsible for bringing the Mercer Girls to Seattle, commenting on his election to the Territorial Legislature by the grateful male constituency

They did it without my spending a nickel. I didn't buy a cigar or a glass of whiskey for anybody.

Captain Ridston
Skipper of the Portland, circa 1897

There, you see those boxes and that safe? Well, they contain in round figures nearly a ton and a half [of gold]. Out of the sixty-eight passengers there is hardly a man on board who has less than $5,000 and one or two have over $100,000.

———

Clarence Berry
Returning home with the reputation
of being the luckiest man in the Klondike

Yes, I have been rather fortunate. Last winter I took out $130,000 in thirty box lengths. A box is twelve x fifteen feet. The second largest nugget ever found in the Yukon was taken out of my claim. It weighed thirteen ounces and was worth $231.
If a man makes a fortune he is liable to earn it by severe hardship and suffering.
But then, grit, perseverance, and luck will probably reward a hard worker with a comfortable income for life.

———

William O. Wood
Upon resigning his office as mayor of Seattle

I'm going to Alaska.

An Old-Timer
Describing Seattle
during the Alaska gold rush
to historian Nard Jones

Nothing on the old Bowery,
before or since, could touch it.
Chicago never had anything like the
gambling, the toughs, the drunkenness,
the women, and the "shows" that you
could see if you wanted . . . San Francisco's
Barbary Coast couldn't touch it, and
I've been along there plenty of times,
too. Hollywood in the 1920s?
To hell with that *fancy* stuff!
I'm talking about standard hell-raising.

~~~~~~~~

Evelyn Hoffman
Historian,
describing a pioneer courtship

One fine day Gilbert [Frost]
rode up to Elizabeth's door
and found her scrubbing the floor.
Without ceremony, he announced
that he had come looking for a wife.
To this she replied, "I'm busy now,
come back tomorrow."
He returned the next day
and she married him.

Archie Binns
Author and historian

The Alaska-Yukon Pacific Exposition
began with a modest scheme to exhibit
Alaska products in a Seattle building
and ended in a World's Fair.
It was an ambitious attempt
for a young city, and it was a success.
The fair made its expenses, and
none of the exhibiting countries
withdrew or declared war on one another.
The city was also on good behavior.
The fair was Seattle's debut among
the cities of the earth,
and Seattle cleaned house so
thoroughly that it was never
again the roaring city
of the gold-rush days.

CHAPTER 11

Will It Play in Seattle?

Frances Farmer
*Celebrated movie star in the 1940s,
wrote this essay as a Seattle high school girl*

God became a super father who wouldn't spank me.
But if I wanted a thing badly enough He arranged it.
That satisfied me until I began to figure out that if God
loved all His children equally, why did He bother
about my hat and let other children lose their fathers
and mothers for always? I began to see that He didn't
have much to do about people's dying or hats or
anything. They happened whether He wanted them to
or not, and He stayed in heaven and pretended not to
notice. I wondered a little why God was such a useless
thing. It seemed a waste of time to have Him. After
that, He became less and less, until He was
nothingness. I felt rather proud to think that I had
found the truth by myself, without help from anyone.
It puzzled me that other people had not found [*sic*] too.
God was gone.

Seattle Times
Headline
following Farmer's first-place prize
from National Scholastic

SEATTLE GIRL
DENIES GOD
AND WINS PRIZE

~~~~~~

Post-Intelligencer
Following Farmer's first movie success,
1940

The big chance in pictures that Frances Farmer,
pretty University of Washington graduate,
had yearned for came with Cinderella-like
unexpectedness just when she had
given up hope of "breaking in."
The Seattle girl had been working
as a foil for other players taking screen tests,
but could not interest producers in her talent.
Discouraged, she was about to leave the
studios and try her luck on the speaking stage.
Then—and it sounds like a fairy tale—
she was "feeding" dialogue to another aspirant
in a test when she attracted the attention
of a director. He recognized her ability at once.
As a result, she was given the ingenue lead in
the forthcoming picture *Too Many Parents*.
And that is Hollywood!

Frances Farmer
Discussing the movie
Rhythm on the
Range

I had no idea what the picture was about all the time I was making it. I never did find out. I was just the tall skinny dame while Bing Crosby and Martha Raye and Bob Burns were having the time of their lives. No one from the front office ever even talked to me about my role. It was a long sweet nightmare for me . . .

Ray Charles
*World-renowned musician
and former Seattle resident*

What do they call this—Bar Mitzvah? Where you
come out as a man? I think Seattle was kind of like that
for me . . . All of a sudden I had to become a man . . .
There were a lot of faces around Seattle, and I tried to
make mine familiar so I could keep working . . .
I could see that in a city like Seattle—
a place which was more sophisticated and open
than I was used to—my act was going to pay off.

~~~~~~~~~~

Elmer Gill
About Ray Charles

He didn't make any special deal about being blind.
He was just one of the boys. He'd walk all over town,
never had a cane. Never used a dog or nothing.
He'd come in always smiling and carrying on.

~~~~~~~~~~

Gaylord Jones
*Seattle musician,
about jitterbugging in 1945*

. . . spectacular. There were tunes
we'd play where I'd be worried
about the floor giving way.
Everybody was really jumping.

Quincy Jones
Songwriter and Seattle native

I must have been fourteen years old and
I wanted to write so badly. I used to listen to
Billy Eckstine's band "Blowing the Blues Away."
I couldn't figure out how eight horns could play
together at the same time and not play the same
note. So Ray [Charles] hit a B-flat seventh in root
position and a C seventh . . . and bang! When I saw
that, it was like the whole world opened up.

———

Ernestine Anderson
Singer and Seattle native

When I went to audition at the Eldorado Ballroom,
the piano player asked me what key did I do these two
songs that I knew in. I automatically said C. It turned
out to be the wrong key so I improvised around the
melody because my grandmother had told me that if
I wanted to be a professional singer, once you start
singing you don't stop. When I finished, one of the
musicians told me I was a jazz singer.

———

John Densmore
*Seattle songwriter and Doors drummer, when asked if
he ever gets tired of hearing the song "Light My Fire"*

I feel a little weird when I hear it in elevators.

Jimi Hendrix
*World-renowned guitarist
and Seattle native*

People see a fast buck and have you up there being a slave to the public. They keep you at it until you are exhausted and so is the public. That's why groups break up—they just get worn out. Musicians want to pull away after a time or they'll get lost in the whirlpool.

Patti Brown
Singer
and Seattle native

When I walked home
from school I passed the
pool hall and the Mardi Gras
and they always had
jazz playing.
My mother was saying no,
but the music said yes.

~~~~~~~~~

Buddy Catlett
Seattle flutist

A lot of people resent
the harshness of the Blues,
an intrusion on the values
they already got set up.
But it's the people in the fields
that bring this culture value.

~~~~~~~~~

Paul Simon
Top-of-the-charts pop singer
and Seattle native

I know when I have a hit because
I hear it on Muzak.

Donny Marrow
Producer of
Seattle's Muzak recordings

Muzak has always reflected contemporary
instrumental music. So in the great musical
revolution of the '60s, anything contemporary
with one's parents was subject to rejection.
Muzak has been bucking a bad image ever
since in spite of the fact that many of
those vocal critics have emerged as
Muzak's happiest customers.

~~~~~~~~~

Bruce Funkhouser
Vice president
of programming at Muzak

Historically,
Muzak has been viewed as Spam.
We'd prefer it to be like Levi's.

~~~~~~~~~

Jon Goforth
Jazz musician
and Seattle resident

I'm alive . . .
and so the problems
continue.

Cameron Crowe
Writer/director of the movie Singles

There's a feeling you get shooting in bigger,
    more cosmopolitan cities where you feel
        like everyone is just there to make
            some money and leave.
        With Seattle, you feel like people
    want to make money and *stay*.
            It's also a sensibility.
                And the air looks different.
                Light looks different.
                It's just crisp, a little more vital looking.
        You can have a shot of someone
            walking down the street;
        and it looks more interesting color-wise
    'cause there's not a lot of haze,
        and the wind's blowing
            and it just feels like . . .
                a haven in some ways.

~~~~~~~~~~

Linda Evans
Actress and former Seattle resident

I didn't want to make a man
the number one quest in my life.
I wanted to make *me*
the number one quest in my life.

Richard Karn
*Seattle resident and actor
from ABC's
"Home Improvement,"
on how he was hired*

Acting is a relative thing. The people who finally get work are those who are better at the business end of things, better at selling themselves. What started in school as a carefree existence turns into something more tenuous and difficult to grasp . . . But I remember summertimes swimming in Lake Washington and boating the San Juans. I remember lots of nights at the Bathhouse Theatre on Green Lake . . . and now I have the brass ring.

Janine Turner
Maggie
in the CBS series
"Northern Exposure"

I've learned to accept myself. I am the person inside and not my body. It's an inside job. Maggie is having a hard time with men, but she keeps trying. Maybe I can learn from her.

Rob Morrow
*Actor who has played opposite Janine Turner
in "Northern Exposure," talking about his costar*

She needs to be connected to civilization.
She surrounds herself with phones, fax machines,
compact disc players, and millions of pictures of her
family and friends and actors she admires as well.

―――――

Joshua Brand
*Co-executive producer of the CBS series
"Northern Exposure," filmed near Seattle,
discussing Barry Corbin, who plays Maurice*

Barry was clearly our first choice. When we wrote
the part we kind of saw George C. Scott in *Patton;*
Robert Duvall in *Apocalypse Now;* John Wayne.
Heroic men of action. Someone who embodied
the best and worst of those American qualities of
capitalism and progress and greed and avarice.

―――――

Barry Corbin
Maurice in "Northern Exposure"

As I explored the character, I discovered
we shared almost nothing in common.
The only thing Maurice is afraid of
is himself. If you took away his shell,
he'd be a quivering mass of ganglia.

Peg Phillips
Storekeeper Ruth-Anne
on "Northern Exposure"

I was an accountant until I was sixty-five.
That's not a bad way to make a living.
But I'm having a lot more fun
now that I'm an actress.
I'm seventy-five and life is good!

Discussing
the "Northern Exposure" cast

It's remarkable how well everybody gets along.
People care about each other. We're a family,
and every family has people that act bratty
sometimes. We're no different.

～～～～～～

Nicole
Nude dancer at Sugar's

I like working with the public . . .
I feel I provide a service.

CHAPTER 12

Grunge and Glory

Geordie Wilson
Social commentator and Seattle journalist

For literature there was Paris in the '20s,
for acid rock and the counterculture movement,
there was the Haight Ashbury in the '60s.
For grunge, of course, there's Seattle.

Jimmy Rowles
*Big-band pianist
and trio recording artist*

To have been able to participate in that
experience in Seattle and learn at the same time
from all these musicians—not be standing around
watching like it is today—I was very lucky.

Marc Ramirez
Pacific magazine music critic,
discussing Eddie Vedder,
the lead singer of Seattle's Pearl Jam

The more successful the band became,
the more Eddie seemed to withdraw.
He was so actual size, so "everyday
gas-attendant normal" that he became
all the more heroic in the eyes of everyday
people everywhere. He wasn't particularly
striking, but there was something about him—
except that now so many teenyboppers have
adopted Eddie as the heartthrob *du jour* that
people have taken to calling the band Girl Jam.
He dons masks in publicity shots.

Chris
From Ten Club,
who handles Eddie Vedder's mail

The typical [fan club] member is between fourteen
and eighteen years old, but letters frequently arrive
from women thirty-five to forty, sometimes
accompanied by photos showcasing lingerie and
swimwear. Like, a lot of them talk about their kids.
They go: "My kids really love your band.
Eddie is really hot." You know, you think
she's writing because her kids are interested,
but it's really because she *wants* Eddie.

Kurt Cobain
Seattle rock star
and founder of the
music group Nirvana,
from his suicide note
to his wife,
Courtney Love

Please keep going,
Courtney, for Frances
[their daughter],
for her life which
will be so much
happier without me.
I LOVE YOU,
I LOVE YOU.

Eddie Vedder
Lead singer of Pearl Jam,
reacting to Cobain's death

They write letters and come to the shows and even to
the house, hoping we can fix everything for them.
But we can't . . . because we don't have all our shit
together either. You can't save somebody from
drowning if you're treading water yourself.

Bob Guccione, Jr.
Editor of Spin magazine,
on Cobain

Rock stars like Kurt are catapulted to
positions of, frankly, exaggerated importance
so quickly that they can no more handle themselves
perfectly than an astronaut can calmly get out of
his seat and walk around while his spaceship is
being propelled into the sky.

Danny Goldberg
Former Nirvana manager,
speaking at Cobain's memorial service

I believe Cobain lived several more years
because of Courtney Love.
When I met him, he was very depressed—his love
for her was one of the things that kept him going.

Susan Faludi
Pulitzer prize-winning author,
on Cobain's widow

What I like about Love is that
    she doesn't just spout the store-bought
      version of feminism.
    Hers is the best kind of feminism
in that it grows out of personal epiphanies
    about the way she's been treated in the culture.
      She's putting together the pieces
    on how the media have jumped on her
for not being a "good mother."
    She understands now why the media
      became preoccupied with her only after
her name was tied up with Kurt Cobain.

———〜〜〜———

Courtney Love
Rock band leader and
Cobain's widow

I'm so embarrassed by this drug history.
    Heroin is not good for the soul.
    You lose the ability to be soulful.
    Something that once acted as an
    aphrodisiac and made everything
      seem so beautiful and gold
      starts to act like a crocodile
      and makes an hour seem
        like a hundred years.

Bruce Pavitt
Cofounder and partner
in Seattle's Sub Pop Records

Ultimately, that which is being
referred to as grunge is going
to be seen as being absolutely
the most ridiculous, obtrusive,
pretentious junk imaginable.
Everybody talks about it,
but nobody knows what it is.
That, to me, is
pop culture at its best.

Bruce Poneman
Cofounder and partner
in Sub Pop Records

We thought
it was very important to
focus on this region and deal
with creative personalities . . .
with a little more anger,
a little more soul,
a little more something to say
because that's what
rock and roll is—
people getting up on the stage
and complaining about
the state of the world.

Patrick MacDonald
Seattle Times reviewer,
on Mudhoney's Seattle homecoming
at the Central

Mark Arm's screaming vocals made the hair
on the back of your head stand up, but most
of the time you could hear [the words]—
gritty, gut-churning images of sickness,
anger and seduction, delivered with fire and
passion . . . gigs like the Central show will be
fondly remembered by fans, because it was
the kind of in-your-face participatory show
you can't get in a theater or coliseum.

~~~~~~

Kit Boss
Seattle Times writer

There thrives in our midst
a cult called Hate. Its headquarters are right
under your nose. . . . The signs of
this Hate cult are subtle yet
unmistakable. There are the
black baseball caps (look for the "HATE" logo).
Also, the T-shirts and buttons
that announce: I LIKE HATE AND I HATE
EVERYTHING ELSE!

Peter Bagge
Creator of the comic book "Hate,"
published in Seattle

My guarantee is that my comic will make people laugh.
I'd like to think there is something a little disturbing
about my comic. There's an edge to it, an
unpleasantness that stays with the
reader and detonates later.

～～～～～

Buddy Bradley
Peter Bagge's antihero,
introducing himself in the premiere issue
of the grunge cartoon "Hate"

. . . So, you've probably heard all about the
glowing reports about how wonderful Seattle is . . .
well let me tell you, it ain't THAT great!
The people act way too PLEASANT and
CIVILIZED. . . makes you wonder what
they're trying to HIDE . . .
Plus it's getting too CROWDED and
POLLUTED . . . Still, I gotta admit it's better
than anywhere else I've been.

～～～～～

Bruce Pavitt
Cofounder and partner in Sub Pop Records

Art is about provoking people.

CHAPTER 13

Culture Still Survives

Sir Thomas Beecham
Symphony conductor, in 1941

If I were a member of this community,
really I should get weary of being looked on
as a sort of aesthetic dustbin.

Vladimir Feltsman
*Concert pianist for the Seattle Symphony
and Soviet émigré*

I love the city [Seattle], and the Market,
where I buy crab. I have a good rapport with
the orchestra. I don't even mind the weather,
the occasional rain. It reminds me of London . . .

Dmitry Sitkovetsky
*Artistic director of
the Seattle International Music Festival*

Fame and accolades are not enough.
A life in music should be a process of self-discovery,
a constant expanding of one's horizons.
Festivals embody this ideal . . .
For my part, it is also a chance to play God a little.

———～———

A. C. Peterson
*Seattle choreographer, discussing Pat Graney, winner
of the American Choreographer Award, whose Seattle-
based company has received worldwide recognition*

A lot of people worry about whether it will be
popular or accepted; Pat doesn't. She gets this
wild idea and just goes for it. The result has
always been work that's interesting to watch.

———～———

Pat Graney
*Discussing the falls her dancers take
in her ballet Sax House*

There's something about the body falling to the floor
that pushes an edge of violence like when you're falling
you're dying, which is sad, or you're sleeping, which is
beautiful. In either case, at some point in the fall you
lose control. It's like total surrender.

CHAPTER 14

The Sporting Life

Colonel Jacob Ruppert
*Owner of the New York Yankees
(as well as a few breweries) to Emil Sick,
owner of the Rainier Brewery,
at a 1938 brewers convention*

Emil, you ought to buy a baseball team.

Emil Sick

Jacob, that's the greatest idea since Repeal.
[Sick went on to buy the Seattle Indians—
which he renamed the Rainiers—
a team that won the Coast League pennant
for three years, cheered by the
largest crowds in the league.]

Green Death
Bicycle Club motto

Eat like a pig,
drink like a pig,
ride like a pig.

~~~~~~~~~~~~~~~~~

Paul Andrews
Cyclist and
Seattle Times technology reporter

The rhythm of a 200-mile bike ride
is something akin to taking
all-day college boards
or driving from
       Seattle to San Francisco.

~~~~~~~~~~~~~~~~~

George Karl
Coach of Seattle's SuperSonics basketball team

The NBA is a lifestyle. I don't think you can be
successful at it unless you are possessed by it. You have
to have this passion to drive yourself, to make the
commitment, to have the discipline, to basically
sacrifice your existence.

Detleff Schrempt
*Veteran forward of the Sonics, commenting
on the team being eliminated in NBA playoff series
after being ranked number one*

We threw eighty-two games away.
We threw away a golden opportunity.
That's what hurt.
Now we have to start over.
We have to play another eighty-two games
to have this kind of chance again.

~~~~~~~~~~

Michael Cage
Sonics' defensive star

To be honest, there are times when I feel like
a man without a country. I mean, in a sense
I'm only going to be a Sonic as long as these
playoffs go on. What valleys can I peek over?
What mountain tops can I set my sights on?
Do I just move back home to San Diego?
Do I pack up everything? It's a weird feeling.
I try to fight it.

The Reverend Dale Turner
*Philosophizing on the occasion of the Sonics
elimination from the NBA championships*

As we grow older, we learn that life can bring both
velvet and sandpaper—some things smooth and lovely
and others rough and difficult. It is a mark of maturity
to both see and deal intelligently with each.

Carlos Rogers
NBA draftee for the Sonics

I was very happy, but it was a definite shock
to be drafted by Seattle. I hadn't even had a workout
with them . . . I love to be part of the Sonics because
all they do is take the ball and run with it.
That's the style of game I play.

Edward Kiersh
Sports magazine writer on Sonics star Shawn Kemp

A mix of youthful exuberance, brilliant ability, and
long-simmering bitterness, Kemp is volatile.
Annoyed by criticism following his alleged
involvement in a stolen jewelry affair, and public
scolding labeling his turning pro "premature,"
he desperately wants to prove himself—not with
rain but with his own brand of deafening thunder.

Shawn Kemp
Sonics superstar player

"Bad, bad, bad boy". . . it lingers on, always there.
I've gotten a lot of criticism. This bothers me, yet
with my making a lot [$30 million for seven years],
I have to expect the attack, I guess . . . Critics like to say
I don't have any $5 million moves, but I'm working 110
percent, and I'm damn tired of hearing what I can't do.

Dallas Malloy
*Seattleite and challenger to the
USA boxing bylaws that forbid her to fight*

I'm constantly being asked to justify what I want
to do because I'm female. I have people asking me,
"Aren't you worried about your pretty face?"
like if I was ugly it wouldn't matter.

Joe Hipp
*Blackfoot tribal member and Seattleite,
ranked fourth by the World Boxing Association*

I just want to be the first Native American
to win the [world heavyweight] title.
The kids [he has three] keep me in my place.
They ask me to tie their shoes or fix the bike . . .
I want people around me I can trust.
I don't go anywhere without my wife.

Trish Bostrom
*Member of Seattle's Husky Hall of Fame
who defeated Billie Jean King at Wimbledon in 1977*

The intense desire to win has not changed
over the years even though physical attributes
of the players have changed dramatically.
When I played I was considered a slightly
taller-than-average player at 5'6". Today
the majority of women players are taller
than 5'9" and the men are primarily 6'
or taller. All are substantially stronger
as well, and the velocity of the game has
dramatically increased with the new composite
racquets. Of the many changes of Wimbledon,
one thing has remained the same. The
strawberries and cream are as great as ever.

Paula Bock
Pacific magazine staff writer

The most efficient way to row—this is where the Zen
comes in—is not to struggle with the water and your
boat but rather to ready yourself to go with the flow.
Never force it. The more you fight the stroke, the
more it will fight back. Soar into the bow like a bird.
Sit like a concert pianist. Think like a ballet dancer.
Reach forward from the hips, flexible, like a mother.
And, most of all—here comes the Zen again—
do nothing.

Corwin Fergus
Seattle Times reporter

No one
I know goes
to Mariner games.
Baseball in Seattle is
a species without a habitat.
The retractable-roof stadium idea
is a poor compromise. If they built a
park south of the Kingdome with seats
facing so I could watch the sunset over the
Olympics and the Mariners, I
would go to
many games . . .
Baseball is a game
of ease and leisurely time
outdoors. People yearn
for this. Serve them
good food while
they have
this experience
and they
will come.

Steve Kelley
Seattle Times sports columnist

. . . Griffey's home runs are becoming
about as occasional as a sunrise,
    and almost as beautiful.
        You know how you might be driving
            on the Alaskan Way viaduct at sunset
and matter-of-factly look west
    and that familiar view of Elliott Bay
        and the Olympic Mountains moves you as if
            you're seeing it for the first time?
    That's what it feels like watching Griffey.
    Everything he does
        we've seen him do before.
In the batter's box and in center field,
    Griffey does it again and again and we watch
    and we're moved all over again.

Dave Niehaus
*Mariners radio announcer
on Ken Griffey, Jr.*

Junior has been very consistent and
has progressed every year.
The question is:
Just what will he be when he's thirty
and has to work at it?
He's making so much money,
you really got to *want* to play the game.

Ken Griffey, Jr.
Seattle Mariners
center fielder,
on why he turned down a
David Letterman interview

I would have had to fly to New York a day ahead of the
team. I wanted to fly there with my teammates . . .
There isn't enough time in the day to talk with
everyone. I try to give the media as much time as I can,
but the media must realize I need my own time.

John Owen
Seattle columnist

In 1961 Sal Durante,
   a Brooklyn truck driver but a Yankee fan,
    caught the ball Roger Maris
     hit for his record-breaking
      61st home run of the season.
    Durante was invited to Seattle—
   expenses paid—to try to catch a baseball
to be dropped off the Space Needle for $1,000.
The accident insurance policy wouldn't
cover Space Needle drops. So Stallard—
who also threw the pitch Maris hit
   for his historic home run—
    tossed the ball off a giant
     Ferris wheel instead.
       (Durante dropped the ball.)

<hr />

Lenny Anderson
Post-Intelligencer columnist

So the Vancouver Canucks are playing
for the Stanley Cup. It took long enough.
The Seattle Metropolitans played
   for the Stanley Cup—
and won it—seventy-seven years ago,
bringing the Pacific Northwest
its first world championship
of professional hockey.

Paula Bock
Seattle journalist

Those Seattle Yacht Club women.
Tall and willowy.
Royal blue and white.
A designer crew that looked
as if they always wore the right clothes,
as if they shopped together,
as if they mail-ordered
thigh cream in bulk,
or, worse yet,
perhaps they were all
born that way,
with those lean muscular legs.
Born to row.

~~~~~~~~

Blaine Newham
Seattle Times columnist

Seattle is an event town,
and Griffey is the main event.

CHAPTER 15

Rain . . .
Who Needs an Umbrella?

Jerry Seinfeld
Comedian
and regular Seattle visitor

Seattle is a moisturizing pad
disguised as a city.

Chicago Tribune

Seattle . . .
The *Moist* Marvel
of Puget Sound.

Richard Eberhard
Poet and Seattle visitor, in 1967

It will stop raining, won't it?

~~~~~~~~~

Jean Godden
Seattle Times columnist

Seattleites never carry umbrellas,
    never wash their cars,
        never shine their shoes,
    never turn on their windshield wipers
until the rain is pouring . . .
    They can describe forty-two shades of gray
        and think a perfect day is 69,
partly sunny, with a breeze from the north . . .
    Real Puget Sounders think we're having
        a heat wave when the thermometer
        reaches 80 degrees.
They feel guilt pangs if they're stuck
    inside on sunny days. And they're still
        looking for sunglasses that were
misplaced the last time we had summer.
    (Was it 1992?)

~~~~~~~~~

Adam Woog
Seattle writer

People in Seattle don't tan—they rust.

T-shirt

Seattle Rain Festival:
January through December.

~~~~~~~~

Bart Becker
Contributing editor, Greater Seattle

The real misconception that outsiders have
about Seattle's rain is that it's a bad, unpleasant thing.
True Northwesterners, on the other hand,
like the misty, foggy weather, with its beautiful
moody promise of regeneration.

~~~~~~~~

E. B. White
Writer
and onetime resident of Seattle

The days here are full of mist
from Puget Sound and of depression.
I find it hard to keep cheerful.

~~~~~~~~

San Francisco Examiner

Seattle is a prim and proper, almost prissy, little city.
It has a scrubbed-clean quality, a result, no doubt,
of one rainstorm after another.

CHAPTER 16
Murder—They Wrote

~~~~~~~~

Earl Emerson
Seattle novelist

I think the rain makes us think about murder.

~~~~~~~~

From Emerson's Deviant Behavior

The house overlooked the Mercer Island
Floating Bridge, the new bridge under construction,
and the green bump that was Seward Park.
In this neighborhood rape-murders happened
about once every fifty years, if that.
I wondered how often there were runaways . . .
The neighborhood was so influential
it had forced Sea-Tac to reroute flight paths.

From Emerson's
Black Hearts and Slow Dancing

A rust-brown smudge
     balloonded over Seattle,
          end to end, a thousand feet thick.
          Mac knew the locals were
telling themselves
     that if they were getting headaches
     and their eyes were bloodshot
     and their noses ran,
          it must be something else.
     Seattleites had a stunning town,
          but it grew dirtier by the minute.
     It was only Northwest
          vanity that kept people
          calling it fog.

~~~~~~~

J. J. Jance
Mystery writer
and Seattle native

I sell books the way I used to
     sell Girl Scout cookies.
     I tell everybody.
     I have signed books in the
meat department of Top Foods.
     I was part of the grand opening
of the Smokey Point Safeway.
It's important for me to meet my readers.

From Jance's *Without Due Process*

By the time we got to the Doghouse parking lot, I was wishing I'd left him to walk, but that was only the beginning. It got worse. I opened the front door of the restaurant to let him go first. He stepped inside, then turned back to me. "My god, it's so smoky in there how can anybody see?"

The Doghouse, smoke and all, is a Seattle institution, but Rankin, as a relatively recent transplant, had clearly never set foot inside the place . . .

"There'd better be a nonsmoking section," Chief Rankin was saying under his breath.

Frederick D. Huebner
Seattle writer

It [Seattle] is a very
cinematic-looking city.
You can manipulate the weather
and the background here because
anything is plausible.

~~~~~~

From Huebner's
Methods of Execution

The Owl Cafe is on lower Ballard Avenue,
south of Market Street, in a neighborhood
of boat brokers, fishermen's bars,
secondhand furniture stores, pawnshops,
and warehouses. I parked on a brick-paved
side street near Shilshole Avenue and
walked the three blocks to the Owl
in a light gathering mist.
The air was thick with the rich rank smells
of the harbor, seaweed and salt and diesel.
I paid six dollars cover to the doorman
and paused in the doorway to let
my eyes adjust to the low lights
and haze of smoke.
Ballard is the last neighborhood
in Seattle where you will not
lose your teeth for lighting
a cigarette in public.

K. K. Beck
Mystery writer and Seattle native

Nowadays my publisher likes the idea of regionalism.
When I first started writing,
almost all mysteries were set in New York or L.A.
My then-agent said, "Oh, for God sakes,
don't write anything about Seattle;
nobody wants to read about Seattle."

———————

From Beck's Amateur Night

The house, on Sunnyside, was a small
cottagy-looking place, set back from the
street with an untidy garden in front. . . .
The old blue-collar element, on in years now,
had favored vinyl siding and updating with
aluminum windows and wrought iron railings.
The new arrivals had encrusted their old houses,
some of them architecturally quite simple,
with lots of lattice, ripped off the fake siding and
replaced it with cedar, and picked out the details
of window trim and gables with interesting color
combinations. They'd also enclosed their gardens
with fences, a reaction, no doubt, to the boundless
contiguous front lawns of their surburban childhoods.
Their gardens went beyond the standard Seattle
collection of ornamental cedars and rhododendrons
with some clumps of heather. They favored clematis
and standard roses and containers full of pansies.

CHAPTER 17

In the Pits over Architecture

R. H. Thompson
*City engineer
responsible for the Denny Regrade,
circa 1900*

Looking at
the local surroundings,
I felt that Seattle was in a pit,
that to get anywhere we
would be compelled
to climb out if we could.

Paul Schell
*Dean of the University of Washington
College of Architecture and
Urban Planning*

It's lack of courage. . . .
We don't want to build
anything too expensive
or that looks too good.
We're afraid of being
too successful.

~~~~~~~~~~

Virgil G. Bogue
City planner, in 1910

Seattle should join the list of cities which have
adopted a limitation of building height—Chicago,
Boston, Washington . . . Minneapolis, and
Los Angeles—and prevent the ills
which unlimited license in this
respect is sure to entail. The majority
of the rooms in skyscrapers require to be
lighted artificially, the sunlight being
shut out, and must also be ventilated
artificially. As a result, they are both
dark and damp, and therefore
breeders of tuberculosis.

Joni Balter
Seattle Times columnist,
about the Kingdome ballpark addition

So you thought the grubworm that attached itself to
the Kingdome was only temporary. Nobody would
put up something that ugly and leave it there, right?
No such luck. . . .

~~~~~~~

Dave Niehaus
Mariners radio announcer

The Kingdome is not a ballpark.
There are no elements, no effect on the baseball.
At Fenway, you can see the grass grow
on some days. Fenway smells,
you can see Ted Williams, Babe Ruth
playing there. I darn near genuflect
when I walk through the gates
at Fenway Park.

~~~~~~~

Mark Tobey
Seattle artist

The Market, not Mount Rainier, is Seattle's soul.